Robot

Claire Daniel
Illustrated by Christine Benjamin

Rigby
A Harcourt Achieve Imprint

www.Rigby.com
1-800-531-5015

Literacy by Design Leveled Readers: *Robot Trouble*

ISBN-13: 978-1-4189-3669-3
ISBN-10:   1-4189-3669-3

Printed in China
3 4 5 6 7 8 985 14 13 12 11 10 09 08

Contents

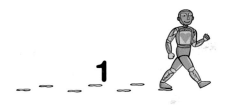

Brava Works!

Gabriela tightened the last screw on the robot's slender, plastic arm, and then she opened the metal panel on its head to study its machine brain one last time. Inside, red, blue, yellow, and green wires twisted together like a pile of string. Carefully pushing the wires aside, she checked the labels on the computer chips underneath to make sure she hadn't left out anything important.

"Math, Science, Following Directions, Dictionary, and Humor," she read aloud.

Gabriela held her breath as she clicked the panel on the robot's head shut. This was the first robot she had ever made, so there was no way of knowing what might happen. Would it come to life? Excited, Gabriela slowly pressed the round, silver "On" button and waited. A red light on the robot's neck blinked, and a green light flashed and then shone steadily.

"Whirrrr, brrrr-umm, brrrr-umm! Ting! Ting!"

After stretching its arms and legs with a jolt and a jerk and a series of squeaks, the robot said, "Brava is ready."

"How are you feeling, Brava?"

"Robots do not feel, Gabriela. However, my systems are in perfect working order, and I am waiting for a command."

Gabriela smiled because it was a good sign that Brava was responding to her voice! Then she looked around at the clothes and books scattered on the floor of her bedroom. She had been working so hard on her robot that she had forgotten to keep her room clean.

"Clean my bedroom," Gabriela commanded. "Pick up the books and stack them on the shelves. Fold the clothes and put them in the drawer."

"Command is received, and I'm happy to follow your orders because this place is a mess!" Brava said excitedly.

Gabriela frowned at Brava, thinking that maybe the Humor program was working *too* well! But the next moment she forgot all about it because she was busy watching Brava's amazingly human-like movements. Brava folded the clothes and shelved the books so swiftly that Gabriela's eyes could barely follow Brava's motions.

After placing the last folded T-shirt into the drawer, Brava turned to Gabriela and announced, "Command has been completed."

Gabriela was about to give Brava another command when a familiar voice asked from the doorway, "What's that?"

Gabriela groaned because the worst thing imaginable had just happened: Her younger brother, Emilio the pest, had discovered Brava!

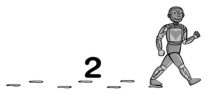

2

Emilio the Pest

"**D**idn't you see the Keep Out sign on my door, Emilio?" Gabriela had thought Emilio was out of the house at soccer practice.

"This is an interesting machine," Emilio said cheerfully, reaching out to grab Brava's plastic arm.

"Don't touch her!" Gabriela ordered him, remembering the many times he had broken her toys when he was younger. "You might break her because you don't know how to make her work."

"What's going to happen if I push this button?" he asked, pointing to the round, silver "On" button.

"That's none of your business," Gabriela told him firmly.

"But it *is* my business," Emilio said, grinning at her. "If you don't show me how this robot works, I'll tell Mom and Dad all about her."

Gabriela frowned because she had hoped to surprise her father with Brava for his birthday this afternoon. Last week Dad had said that she wouldn't be able to go to Space Camp because she hadn't signed up in time. Dad had been told that the program was already full. But Gabriela was busy dreaming up another way to be at the Space Center this summer. Maybe if she showed Dad that she could build a perfectly working robot, she could convince him to give her a job at the Space Center with him.

"OK, I'll tell you, but you can't let Mom and Dad know about her until I'm sure she's ready," she warned Emilio.

"I won't say anything," he promised.

"She follows my commands, and her brain is programmed to know about school subjects so that she can help me with my homework," Gabriela explained. "Her name is Brava, and you can say hello to her."

"Please do say hello, little brother, the pest," Brava encouraged him.

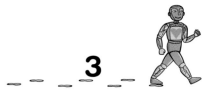

3

A Soapy Mess

"**S**he talks funny, but she's amazing!" Emilio said.

"Well, what did you expect?" Brava inquired politely. "After all, I was built by a genius."

"Oh, no!" Emilio laughed. "I think we might have to reprogram some parts of her brain."

"I am waiting for a command," Brava told him.

"Wash and rinse everything in the kitchen sink," Emilio said, thinking of the lunch dishes that his mother had asked him to wash.

"You have to tell Brava exactly what to do," Gabriela corrected him. "Brava, wash the oil and grease off everything that is in the sink. After you rinse off each dish, put it into the drain rack."

Down in the kitchen, Brava began washing the dishes, rinsing each one clean, and then carefully putting it into the drain rack. She seemed to understand the task. Just then they spotted their mother through the window. She was coming toward the back steps, carrying a red rose.

"Hurry! We can't let Mom see Brava!" Gabriela shouted, running to the door.

When she reached her mother, Gabriela hugged Mom's arm and said, "I love that beautiful red rose you picked, Mom! Let me take it and put it in a vase for you."

"OK," her mother said, confused by Gabriela's excitement over the flower.

"And will you let me weed the garden?" Emilio asked. "I've been wanting to do that for a long time!"

Mom seemed puzzled, since Gabriela and Emilio had never shown any interest in the garden before. Still, she followed Emilio back to the garden and handed him a shovel.

While Mom stayed in the garden with Emilio, Gabriela rushed back into the kitchen and stared at Brava in horror. The robot stood bent over the kitchen sink as still as a stone.

4

Too Much Hair

It took Gabriela over an hour to fix Brava, but Emilio helped her, so the work went quickly.

"I think I gave her bad directions," Gabriela said as Emilio dried Brava's arms with a big, fluffy towel. "I told her to wash everything in the sink that was oily. Brava is oily, so she must have decided to wash herself, too! Then the soapy water broke her motor, and she stopped working."

"We'll just have to be more careful next time," Emilio said.

"Now we'd better think of a simple command to give Brava to make sure that she's working correctly again," Gabriela said, once they had put Brava's front panel back on.

Emilio remembered that this morning their mother had been complaining about how much hair their dog, Oliver, was leaving around the house.

"If Brava brushes Oliver, Oliver won't shed as much," Emilio suggested.

"Good idea!" Gabriela agreed, "Go get the dog."

When Oliver saw Brava, the dog started barking loudly.

Brava said, "Do not be scared, Oliver. I may be a robot (not a human being), but you should not worry. I promise not to hurt you."

"Brava, my command for you is to brush the dog," Gabriela said very slowly and clearly.

"Tell Brava why she should brush the dog, Gabriela," Emilio suggested. "Good directions will help her brush him the right way."

Gabriela explained, "Oliver sheds a lot, but if you brush him, he won't leave hair all over the place."

Oliver whined and moved to the corner, not happy at all about being brushed by a robot!

"Do not worry, little doggie, I will be gentle," Brava promised Oliver, softly brushing his coat.

Just then Gabriela's mother called up the stairs, "Gabriela, did you remember to clean up the living room for your father's birthday today?"

Gabriela frowned because she had, in fact, forgotten about cleaning the living room. She thought about asking Brava to do it, but she couldn't think of a way to sneak the robot downstairs without Mom seeing her. Then Gabriela looked at Emilio, who was watching Brava brush the dog. Huge clumps of golden dog hair floated to the floor with each stroke.

"Don't leave this room," she ordered Emilio and went downstairs to help her mother clean the living room.

After Gabriela finished cleaning, she ran back upstairs to see how things were going. She swung the door to her room open and shrieked at what she saw inside. Hearing the noise, Emilio looked away from the game he was playing on the computer, and then he shrieked, too. Oliver, completely bald, blinked in confusion from where he lay on the floor, next to an enormous pile of dog hair.

5

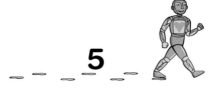

A Special Recipe

"**Y**ou were supposed to be watching Brava, Emilio! How could you let her shave all the hair off the dog?"

"I didn't notice what she was doing because I was playing my game. What good is a robot if you can't leave it alone, anyway?"

Gabriela knew Emilio was right, and said, "I guess we will have to work harder at giving better directions. Brava, you need to pay attention when I give you directions."

Brava explained, "I always do. You said the dog had too much hair, so I removed the hair. Now there will be much less dog hair around the house. Don't you agree?"

Gabriela wanted to laugh, but she didn't have time. "The birthday party for Dad is in only a few hours, Emilio. What can we tell Brava to do to keep her out of trouble until then?"

25

"Dad loves chocolate cake, so have Brava make him a chocolate birthday cake from the recipe that Mom uses," Emilio suggested.

"That's a great idea, but we have to make sure to give Brava very good directions this time," Gabriela warned her brother.

Down in the kitchen, Gabriela read the recipe aloud to Brava, being careful to say each word very slowly and clearly. Afterwards she looked at Emilio and asked, "Did I say everything correctly?"

Emilio nodded, and Gabriela said to Brava, "Remember, Brava, the ingredients you need to use are sugar, chocolate, butter, flour, eggs, milk, salt, vanilla, and baking soda."

"Right, I will need sugar, chocolate, butter, flower, eggs, milk, salt, vanilla, and baking soda," Brava repeated.

Suddenly they all heard Mom's voice calling from the porch, "Kids, come get in the car so we can all go pick up Dad!"

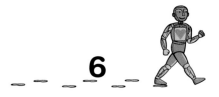

6

Chocolate and Roses

Emilio ran outside, and Gabriela told Brava, "You have about an hour and a half to mix and bake the cake before we all get back. When you're done, take the cake to my room and hide it."

"Command is received," Brava told Gabriela.

Once everyone had left, Brava began gathering together the ingredients for the cake. Spotting Mom's red rose on the kitchen table, Brava said, "Gabriela told me to use a cup and a half of flower, but I do not think this one flower is enough to make a cup and a half."

So Brava walked out into the garden and cut several of the rose blooms off one of Mom's rose bushes. Humming happily to herself, she carried the blooms inside and put the rose petals into a bowl with the rest of the ingredients. She made her hand spin very quickly around and around, mixing everything together.

Brava then poured the mixture into a metal cake pan and carefully placed the pan into the oven. After ten minutes, she smelled the mixture baking. However, when she peered inside the hot oven, she was disappointed to see that the cake looked soupy.

Then she had an idea and said, "A much better way to bake would be to turn the oven up so that the cake will bake faster!" After baking the cake at a hotter temperature for five more minutes, Brava flipped the cake out of the pan onto a plate. Then she used green icing to write "Happy Birthday!" on top.

"Now the cake and I must wait in Gabriela's room," Brava told Oliver, passing by him as she climbed up the stairs. "This cake turned out so well that everyone will be very pleased. Don't you agree?"

Dad's Birthday Surprise

When the family's car pulled up into the driveway, Gabriela's mother cried out, "What happened to my beautiful rose bush?"

All of the rose blooms had been cut off, and the bare ends of the stems were sticking up into the air. Gabriela and Emilio looked at one another with concern because they were sure that Brava must have had something to do with this.

But when the family walked inside, nothing seemed wrong. Brava hadn't left a mess in the kitchen. Still talking about her poor rose bush, Mom started handing food from the refrigerator to Gabriela. Meanwhile, Dad and Emilio began to set the table. Both children wanted to go upstairs and check on Brava, but their parents kept them too busy downstairs.

Once they were all eating dinner, Gabriela said excitedly, "Dad, Emilio and I have a surprise for you."

While Emilio went upstairs to get Brava, Gabriela prepared her parents to meet the robot. "Dad, I made something to show you that I've got the skills to get a job at the Space Center with you. I may be too young, but I'm smart, and I like to work hard and . . ."

Before Gabriela could finish her sentence, Emilio walked into the kitchen, followed by Brava, who was carrying a very flat-looking cake.

"Wow, what is that amazing thing?" Dad said with wide eyes.

Brava marched across the floor to him and said, "My name is Brava, and I am a robot." Gabriela's father opened his mouth to speak, but no words came out.

Proudly placing the cake in front of Dad, Brava informed him, "Here is a cake for your birthday that I made for you all by myself."

8

A Surprise for Gabriela

Gabriela thought the cake didn't look quite right because it was very flat, and there were strange-looking red things sticking out of it. Then she remembered the recipe, and she realized that Brava must have confused the word *flour* with the word *flower!*

Quickly she shouted, "Wait, Dad, don't eat . . ."

But it was too late because Dad had already cut himself a piece and begun chewing. "That's the best fudge I've *ever* tasted," he told everyone, cutting himself another piece, "and the rose petals are a great birthday surprise!"

"It is cake, not fudge," Brava corrected him. "I turned the oven up to a hotter temperature and baked it very quickly while you were all gone."

"Baking the cake that hot turns it into a kind of fudge," Mom explained to Brava, laughing. "But you are a very good baker, even if you did take petals from my rose bush."

"Brava can help you grow new roses in your garden, Mom," Gabriela told her mother while everyone cut themselves pieces of the delicious fudge. "And can I come and work at the Space Center with you, Dad? I made Brava, and she works pretty well—even if she does make some mistakes."

"I only make mistakes when I am given incorrect directions," Brava told Dad.

Gabriela's father laughed and said, "She is a wonderful machine, but I'm afraid that I can't give you a job at the Space Center. You are still too young to work there."

Gabriela's eyes filled with tears, but then her father added, "But I do have good news for you and Emilio. Two of the Space Camp students dropped out of camp, so now there's room for two more!"

Gabriela was too excited to say anything, but Brava said happily, "This is wonderful news, Gabriela, because maybe at Space Camp you will learn how to give better directions!"

Everyone laughed, and Gabriela groaned, "I guess I'll have to figure out how to fix Brava in my spare time."

But Dad just picked up another piece of fudge and replied, "Actually, I like this robot just the way she is!"